African Serval Cats as Pets

General Info, Purchasing, Care, Cost, Keeping, Health, Supplies, Housing, Grooming, and More Included!!

By Lolly Brown

Foreword

Are you a cat lover? The African Serval cat may pique your interest. It is a super sleek cat characterized by its long legs and lean body. The African Serval cat has a small head, a long neck and a short tail. African Serval cats are often referred to as giraffe cats because of its appearance.

These amazing cats are found in grassy homes in the savannas of Africa. The African Serval cats are crepuscular animals—they are active during dawn and dusk. They evade the heat of the day. They are neither nocturnal nor diurnal, but when it is necessary, they sometimes hunt during night time. African Servals are marvelous hunters—they hunt twice as fast and as successful compared to the other wild cats. Their prey includes frogs, crabs, birds, reptiles, fish, large insects and small rodents. The long legs of the African Serval cats allow it to jump almost 3 meters off the ground, making it easy for them to catch a bird even when it is in flight. Their long legs also allow them to reach deep into burrows for a meal. Moreover, they are equipped with sonic hearing. They can hear high-pitched sounds that come from their prey. These incredible cats can also snatch frogs and fish out of the water by using their curved claws. On the other end, the African Serval cat needs to be wary of hyenas, wild dogs and predators. They use their super speed and the ability to climb trees to escape bigger animal—even people—that are a threat to them.

Georges - Louis Leclerc, Comte de Buffon—a French naturalist in the 1800s—notes that the African Serval cat is very, very fast and can cover a short distance in a short span of time, as if it appears and disappears! He describes the Serval cat as resembling the cat in terms of figure and resembling the tiger because of its black and white spot on its hair. Moreover, the African Serval cat is different from the other members of the cat family in that it loves to play and leap in the water. It is quite a unique feline.

In this book, you will not only discover incredible information about the African Serval, how it lives in the wild and its conservation status, you will also find out if this unusual exotic cat is great for a pet.

Table of Contents

Chapter One: All About the Unique African Serval Cats

Deep within the savannas in southern and Central Africa, where there are mighty rivers and densely -planted streams, you will find most African serval cats. They are medium-sized cats, topping at most at 40 pounds. They look like caracals, which are their competition for prey; only the African serval cats are taller and more slender. They top out at 18 kilograms but most common adult African serval cats range from 9 to 13 kilograms in weight. The African servals, endemic to Africa, thrive on wet areas all over the sub-Saharan Africa, in grasslands and deep forests where there are lush patches of vegetation and waterways. They flourish where there are water sources and do not inhabit deserts and central tropical rainforests.

The name of the African serval cat is taken from the Portuguese word *cervus* which means deer; that is the serval cat is a "deerlike wolf". In Africa, where the servals are unique to, they are commonly called "bush cats". In the African language, Afrikaans, these incredible cats are called *tierboskat* or tiger bush cat.

How does an African serval cat look like and how can you distinguish them from the other wild cats in the African savannah? You will know one when you see one, they are not hard to miss! Because one of the most distinguishing factors that make an African serval cat stands out are its big ears. Their ears are so big and round, that you won't miss them. They are set very close together. Just imagine, if human's ears were the same proportion to their heads as the

African serval cats' are, then human ears would be as big as dinner plates! Another distinguishing feature of the serval cat is its elongated neck, earning it the nickname "giraffe cat".

This lean-built cat stands about 20 inches at the shoulders. The body of the African serval cat is slim and its legs are quite long for the size of its body. The legs can be up to 3 feet long! The African serval cat's legs are considered the longest among all the wild cats in terms of proportion to the body. The African serval cat sports a short tail that has a black tip and about six to seven black rings. The tail is only a third of the whole body length of the serval. Its coat pattern varies, but the most common coat color is pale yellow covered with spots of different sizes. Often the spots merge together and form into vertical stripes along the serval cat's neck and back. The underbelly of this cat is a similar pale color as its coat, only lighter than its coat and also has spots. Some servals have coats that are golden brown or black in color, and they also sport spots or stripes through their dark coat.

African serval cats produce a variety of vocalizations including growling, snarling, purring, and spitting. They can also give out a high-pitched cry when they want to call the attention of other servals. An African serval cat will arch its back and growl loudly when there is the need to defend itself. They are wary of leopards, hyenas and wild dogs that can chase and eat them. But they can escape these predators by running very fast and climbing tall trees.

African serval cats can live in the wild up to 11 years and up to 20 years in captivity.

The social interaction of the male and female serval cats are not long—it only happens seasonally when breeding and during short periods of traveling and resting together. During seasons when female servals are in heat, their social interaction with males is much longer and more frequent. Female serval cats can produce litters of 3 to 4 throughout the year. The serval kittens are born among underbrush or in thick grass covers. Usually, female servals give birth during the end of summer, and the gestation period is from 65 to 77 days. Within 9 to 12 days, the eyes of the kitten will open and after three weeks, they are ready for solid food. It is interesting to note that the mother serval will raise its young, called kittens, by herself, going away frequently to hunt for food. The father does not have any active parenting role. When the male serval cubs are old enough to hunt by themselves, usually at 6 to 8 months, the mother will drive them away from the lair.

The female cubs will stay with their mothers until they grow old enough to be sexually mature. It is only at this time they will leave their homes—forced out is more like it—and set up their own territories. They mark their territories with scent from feces and urine and usually, the serval homes range from 15 to 25 square meters wherein the other serval cats try to avoid contact. While both genders of serval cats mark their territories, males do so more frequently than females and spray their area about 45 times in an hour! Females only do so with half as much time.

Traditionally, there are about 18 subspecies of the serval cat, but the recent taxonomic revision only recommends three: *Leptailurus serval lipostictus* of East Africa, *Leptailurus serval serval* of Southern Africa and *Leptailurus serval constantina* of West and Central Africa.

The African serval cat, much like the cheetah, hunts and goes about the savannas alone. It is a solitary creature, except during mating time or when the female is taking care of its young. They are also found to be tolerant with same-sex servals, but still respect territories. The serval cat is a carnivore and it possesses a very unique behavior when it comes to hunting—it pounces. A serval cat will stun its prey in surprise by leaping into the air and landing on its prey using its powerful forepaws. With their relatively long legs, they have the uncanny ability to leap vertically, making it hard for their prey to run away. The diet of the African serval includes rats, rodents, birds, insects, frogs, fish, crabs, and small reptiles. Not only is a serval successful at pouncing, it also uses its sharp claws to snatch small animals from their burrows or hooking fish or crab right out of the water.

African serval cats are crespuscular creatures — relatively active during dawn and dusk. These animals are timid and elusive. While they do not have the benefit of daylight to help during hunting, they are at an advantage because they have an excellent hearing ability and can detect their prey movements, even when it is underground. They will crawl up quietly to the prey's location and pounce on it. They can even use echo to pick on the vibrations made by their prey or predator. As with any cat, African servals play with their prey before they eat it. But it's not really about "playing with their food" — servals will rain down blow upon bow on their prey using their paws so that they will kill or stun them before they will even try to take a bite. They are smart animals and won't risk their safety. Some African serval cats may hunt during the night or during the day, especially when they are feeding their cubs or it is the wet season. They will escape from the heat by resting under shady bushes or deserted aardvark holes.

The African serval cat is not very popular in Africa as it is rarely seen. However, even though it is seldom spotted, its distribution across Africa is on a decline. Conservation plans are being set in place to address the principal threats that plague the African serval cats. The African serval cats are being hunted for sport, meat, skin tribal clothing, ceremonial purposes and medicine. African serval cats are easily hunted. They are usually chased by dogs, causing them to run up a tree. When they are high up, they can easily get shot, sometimes for game, sometimes for revenge. Most farmers in South Africa believe that serval cats take sheep and poultry; however, it is likely the fault of the jackal and the caracal.

On top of hunting, the loss of habitat due to burning of grasslands, draining of wetlands, overgrazing, and human invasion are also great factors that have caused tremendous impact on the numbers of these extraordinary felines. When the wetland is drained, the rodent densities decline in the areas where African serval cats live. Similarly, the servals won't thrive in places where there is less grass.

They will only live in agricultural areas that have plenty of water and ample covering of grass. Add the pet trade into the mix and the beautiful African serval cat is really a prime target for poachers.

African serval cats are known to breed well in captivity. In fact, they live longer when they are not in the wild. So far, only the North African serval cats are considered by the IUCN Red List as endangered. The other species of serval cats are under the "least concerned" category.

Chapter Two: Caring for an African Serval Cat as a Pet

Do you think that owning a serval cat is something new? Not really. Since ancient Egyptian times, servals have been kept in homes. This, however, doesn't mean that African serval cats are entirely domesticated. Over a hundred years ago, the first servals arrived in the United States and they have been bred through many generations of imports from Africa. The African serval cat is a lovely animal to keep as a pet. This exotic wild cat can be owned through a breeder or your big cat sanctuary. There are domestically - bred serval cat species. Some are easy to tame and care for, others not so. Nevertheless, there are many restrictions and prohibitions when it comes to owning one. Should you decide to take one home, you will have to prepare for and consider the following:

1. **Permit and license**

   This is the first thing you must secure. You cannot own an African serval cat, or any exotic pet for that matter, without first getting permission. Owning exotic pets can be illegal in some states so you should be aware of these things. Your local government will require you to get inspections, permits and licenses that are applicable with the law. Check with your local laws before you decide to buy or rescue a serval cat.

2. **A huge and secure enclosure that is outdoors**

   A male African serval cat usually weighs 20-40lbs while a female serval can weigh from 15-26 lbs. The serval can grow to a height of 21 to 26 inches. These are big cats. They won't thrive in small enclosures. Moreover, they are expected to live for up to 20 years in captivity so you best make sure to provide a secure and comfortable home for them in the next two decades. You need a big space where your highly active serval cat can run around for up to about four miles every day.

If you have a wide space outdoors, make sure that it is enclosed so that your serval cat won't have the chance to escape. Keep in mind that they are great hunters—the best, actually—and they are great at hiding and finding ways to have their own way. Your enclosure should also closely resemble an African serval's natural habitat, savannas or grasslands. There should be plenty of lush greens and water sources. Servals love to swim. Having a small pool of water is best. The serval will go to it for swimming and drinking. And remember, they won't rink from a water dish! You can even place fish in it for your cat to hunt. The African serval loves tall grass and bushes. It prefers to hide its tail and will seek the cover of tall grass to hide from its prey in preparation for a pounce. It also likes to climb on trees.

African serval cats are solitary creatures that would like to have their own territory of approximately 5 to 12 square miles. And remember, even if you put a fence around its enclosure, African servals love to dig and they can go under the ground to escape—unless it jumps over or climbs the fence! Hence, the enclosure should be totally fenced in.

3. **A warm environment**

African serval cats are native to Africa, in savannas where the climate is tropical and there is enough water. It won't thrive well in cold climates. If you live in a state where you experience cold winters or other harsh weathers, then you may not be able to bring home an African serval with you.

4. **Plenty of prey to hunt and feed on**

It is inherent for African serval cats to hunt. They won't just sit back and wait for you to serve them their meow chow on food dishes. They like to look for their food and work for their food. And it is good for them—not only will it satisfy their natural instincts, it will also give them good physical and mental exercise. They love to hunt in places where they can stay near water sources—not a water dish, though—and hide so they can hunt. They will feed on rodents, small fish, large insects, etc. You need to be creative about releasing these small animals that your African serval can hunt for. Your African serval can even catch a bird in flight up to nine feet above in the air. They also love to dig under the ground for their food.

5. **Veterinary care from an exotic animal veterinarian**

Exotic animals may require special care. They will encounter different health issues that cannot be dealt with by your regular, general vet. Make sure that you have an exotic animal vet in your area or you have easy access to one in case you need to bring your African serval cat in for routine checkup or for emergencies. Learn more about serval cat nutrition and health issues in the succeeding pages.

Feeding Pet Serval Cats

The diet of your pet African serval cat requires more nutrients compared to the diet of a domesticated small cat. This is because in the wild, the serval will feed on a lot of protein sources. If they are in captivity, these nutritional requirements must be met. For example, they also need a good dose of calcium, 54mg, while they are still kittens. In the wild, they get calcium from the bones of their prey. That is why you cannot satisfy your pet serval with only pre-cut flesh or simple kibbles.

Your pet serval cat will need the following in its diet: raw meat, fish and bone-in poultry. These meats should be supplemented with the appropriate vitamins required for wild cats. You can give your African serval cat the following:

- Beef (you can offer any cut of beef as well as ground beef)
- Chicken (give all parts such as legs, thighs, neck, wings, quarters. You can also give ground chicken)

- Turkey (give necks and ground turkey)

- Canned fish such as mackerel, salmon and tuna

- Vegetables like tomatoes and lettuce

- Fruits such as oranges, strawberries, cherries, bananas

- Treats like beef jerky and cheese

If your pet is still a kitten, you need to give it fine foods instead of whole foods. Your serval kitten will need ground raw meat that is mixed with wet food. Most of the cat food available in the market is not suited for serval cats. If you are going to give kibble, make sure that they are of the premium kind and 75% meat-based. Your kitten can also chew on a chicken wing when it is already 6 weeks old. Be careful when giving canned diet as some servals have been known to develop stones because of the high salt content of cat food in cans.

Mature serval cats will be able to eat a whole chicken neck or chicken leg. When you give chicken to your serval cat, remove the skin as this will make your cat fat. Never feed your African serval cat with cooked meat, always give it raw ones. As your serval cat matures, it can eat chicken with bones in it. This is good because the phosphorus and calcium they need can be found in animal bones. If your pet serval lacks these nutrients, its own bones can become brittle and it will have other illnesses.

Your adult African serval cat will need 1 to 3 pounds of meat in one day. You can also provide a feeding of grass to your serval cat at least once a week. Eating grass helps these cats have a healthy digestive system. Some days your cat will eat a lot and the some days it won't—that is normal. However, when your serval cat consistently eats very little to no food, you should get veterinary attention. They may be lacking vitamins needed that will boost their appetite. Your pet serval cat needs clean water daily. Putting several water dishes around your house so that your cat can have easy access to drinking water Change it daily and check to see if it becomes dirty—the serval cat will not drink from a dirty water source and if it doesn't, it could get dehydrated.

As a reminder, you should always keep your toilet lids down. The serval cat loves to play with water and it could drown in your toilet bowl. A better option is to keep your bathroom door closed, so that your serval cat will not have access to the chemical cleaners you use in your toilet.

Playing with an African Serval Cat

It has been said over and over in this book — serval cats are very active and very playful. Your pet will love to pay fetch with you and will always bring you things to throw. They love to retrieve things and jump high to catch them. You will be long tired playing fetch but your pet serval will still have so much energy running and jumping about.

The serval cat loves playing with water, unlike most domesticated cats or even other big cats, so when you leave your shower door open, you will most likely see it there with you as you take a shower. If you can put a small kiddie pool outside of its enclosure, your pet serval will always get a dip.

If you have more than one serval cat at home, be prepared to stay up late at night because they will chase each other and play all around your house, leaping on furniture and bouncing on walls.

You can provide your African serval cat with a variety of toys. While it is still a kitten, you can purchase the cat toys made for domesticated cats. When your serval cat matures, the toys can be too small for them and they can easily destroy them by chewing on or clawing at them. If the toys you provide are too small or they get chewed off, your serval cat may risk ingesting small pieces. They can either choke or have intestinal problems. Instead, you can purchase pet toys made for medium and large dogs.

Bonding with a Serval Cat and Other Concerns

Usually, serval cat owners get kittens that they can raise and hand-feed or bottle-feed. This is important because African serval cats can develop a bond with their human owners and this one-human relationship can stay for life. It is also a risk, because when the time comes that you cannot keep your serval with you anymore, for whatever reason, then you will have a problem as they don't take lightly to

having new owners. They will stick to their one-human
bond.

When you bond with your kitten, you will have to
spend time playing with it. Always keep it at eye level. You
will have to exercise a lot of patience and gentle handling,
especially when training your cat. You can litter-train your
serval cat, but still expect it to pee all around as it marks its
territory. It is not trying to rile you up, it is a natural instinct.
Remember that a serval cat will not be too excited to meet
other people or other pets. They are solitary and shy and
will shun other interaction apart from yours. They can be
afraid of strangers and visitors, so never force your cat to
"meet" someone else.

The serval cat is active at night—this means that you
will have to dedicate some parts of your night to bond with
it, or to accept that you cannot keep it still while you sleep. If
your serval will be housed within your home while it is a
kitten, then you should baby-proof the room so that your cat
won't break anything and it won't get hurt.

While most small domesticated cats can be quite affectionate, the level of affection that your serval cat can show is at best medium. It is rarely kid-friendly. It won't even be too friendly with adults. It is also not very forthcoming with your other pets that you may have at home. Don't expect it to jump for joy and play with your other household pets.

On the other hand, the African serval cat has a high need for exercise. It will always want to move its long legs by jumping and pouncing. It has a very high level of energy and playfulness. And even if it is a cat that loves to play, it doesn't really like to be taught. It has a low trainability level despite its high intelligence. In the wild, it will use its cunning skills to survive and thrive, but don't expect it to use its high IQ to learn tricks from you.

The African serval cat has a moderate tendency to vocalize. It will growl when it is in a playful mood or when it is scared or is trying to scare someone off. You won't easily know it unless you have spent quite some time with it, to understand its vocalizations. A high-pitched call from your

African serval may mean it is in pain or it is calling out other servals. Like most domesticated cats, you will also hear your serval purr and make spitting noises.

Do you want to take your serval cat for a walk? You can do so. But you may need a special harness as serval cats are much stronger than regular domesticated cats. You don't want it to drag you or get away from you when it starts to run off and chase something it perceives as prey.

If you plan on traveling, you may not always be able to bring your serval cat with you, unlike a small domesticated cat that you can place in a cage. You should put your African serval with someone who can care for it while you are on a vacation or whatever reason you need to go away.

Keep in mind that it doesn't take well with new owners or new people taking care of it. Make sure to keep both your cat and the person caring for it safe by planning measures beforehand. You can place the serval cat in its enclosure so that it won't have contact with your friend who is taking care of it. The person should just monitor if the cat is safe and doesn't encounter safety or health issues.

Common Health Concerns of Serval Cats

African serval cats are exotic creatures that require exotic care from a specialized animal doctor. If there is no exotic animal veterinarian in your area, you may have to think twice before bringing home a serval cat. Some issues that require specialized vet care including the following:

1. **Regular Pet Care:** An African serval cat will need deworming as well as annual immunizations.

2. **Declawing:** When it comes to declawing, it has been mentioned beforehand that while it can be "safe" for the owner and those living with him in the beginning, declawing can be quite disadvantageous to your cat in terms of hunting for its food and protecting itself. Furthermore, declawing can bring about an infection.

3. **Emergency Care:** As serval cats like to chew and eat, they are prone to ingesting stuff that they shouldn't. Foreign objects can cause choking, stomach problems, and even poisoning.

Poor Nutrition

Oftentimes, a serval cat may have problems because of poor nutrition. Your exotic pet veterinarian can give you proper advice on what to give your serval cat to keep them healthy and far from illnesses. Finding the best diet for your African serval can prove to be an arduous task. In the wild, their natural diet consists of a wide variety. In captivity, it can be limited—and this is where you have to be careful.

While you may not have access to everything your African serval cat can have in the wild, you can get rodents, birds, insects, fish, frogs and small reptiles and offer it as part of its diet. Your African serval will need these protein sources to fuel it energy.

Moreover, you cannot give it dead meat. The African serval will thrive on hunting and killing its own food. You cannot offer it sliced meat on food dishes or tie a rat or rabbit by its foot, it just won't do. Your intelligent serval cat will want to forage for its own food. It is better to find a puzzle of food game that will offer enrichment to your cat, in terms of nutrition and mental health. The more joy and challenge your cat gets from foraging its own food, the healthier it will be. Sometimes, when your serval cat catches a prey, it will eat everything so fast only to regurgitate. Don't fret; it is normal for your serval cat to do so.

Always provide clean water, as your serval cat will use the water in its small pool for both drinking and swimming. On top of a rich variety of protein sources and clean water, your exotic pet veterinarian will suggest that you give carnivore supplement to your serval cat. This feline supplement can be added to its food.

You can get and offer your African serval cat a pelleted diet, especially if it has been raised by humans and hand-fed or bottle-fed since birth. However, to fulfill its basic instinct, your pet's diet should not be limited to a pelleted meal.

Weight Management

A lot of pet owners love to feed their pet serval cats— and this could lead to obesity. Obese cats are at risk of suffering from a number of illnesses and even death. You should be careful about ignoring the extra weight that your serval cat puts in. While you think it may look cute, it can lead to the development of diabetes, arthritis or other diseases that can threaten the life of your pet.

Even with people, shedding a few pounds can bring about great health benefits, and it is the same with your serval cat. A fat African serval cat may have a reduced lifespan. Being overweight can also lead to fatty liver and hepatic lipidosis—these can be fatal to your cat.

Make sure that you keep your African serval cat's weight normal. A trim cat is a healthy cat. Your serval should eat enough every day, roughly about 5 to 10 times a day with just a few bites. You can try free feeding, but this can also lead to boredom and make your cat skip meals. Get some food puzzles o they can forage. Ask your vet for the right amount of food that you serval cat needs for its age as well as the ideal weight so that you know how much food you need to give it on a daily basis.

When you need to regulate your serval cat's food intake, you need to be tough. Your pet can be affectionate and ask you for food but you need to be firm about it. Instead of giving it food, youc an engage it with other activities such as playtime or be affectionate with it. When you ignore its pleading for extra food, it will also ignore you, so get ready to lose some personal interaction, too, until your cat gets used to its diet. By playing with it instead of giving it food, pretty soon, your cat will forget about eating and just love spending with you. Not only will its physical body be healthy, its mind and emotions will be healthy, too.

Dental Diseases and Gum Problems

Your serval cat can suffer from inflammation of the gum tissue. This usually happens in the area that surrounds the molar teeth. To prevent this, your serval cat's teeth should be brushed daily. If it already suffers from swollen gums, get the medical attention of a qualified vet. Your serval cat will need this extra help from you as it cannot clean its own teeth effectively. Brushing will help remove food residue and prevent dental disease from occurring or progressing. Preventive care is always better.

Infections that are Vaccine - Preventable

As with all cats, Africa serval cats are prone to bacterial and viral infections including rabies, panleukopenia, rhinotracheitis, and calicivirus. All these can be prevented by having your serval cat vaccinate. These core vaccines are highly recommended and actually needed. Further, you can also opt to get vaccines to protect your serval cat from other dangerous diseases such as the FeLV or feline leukemia virus. Always ask your qualified vet what kind of vaccines your cat needs. It is dependent on the age of your cat, the prevalent diseases in your locality and other health factors.

Heartworm Infection

Parasitic infection has no treatment. The best practice is to prevent your serval cat from acquiring this fatal illness. All kinds of parasites can attack your African serval cat—inside its body and outside. Fleas, mites and ticks can infest and irritate your serval cat's ears and skin. In its digestive system, roundworms, whipworms, hookworms and heartworms can thrive. These parasites can be ingested through dirty drinking water. They can also go inside your serval cat's body as it walks on contaminated soil. Another way parasites can get in your cat's body is through mosquito bites.

Parasitic infection is a serious issue because the parasites can also infect your family members. For your African serval cat, the effects can be discomfort, pain, and death. Make sure that your pet serval is tested for parasites through a fecal exam. There is also preventative medication.

Now that you are interested in serval cats, you should also brush up on your knowledge and research more in detail. You can go join exotic big cat organizations, talk to reputable breeders, or connect with other serval cat owners to find out more about this amazing cat that you want to call your pet. By understanding what your pet needs and how you can make life more exciting for it, you will be able to give it a good life and enjoy its company in return.

Chapter Three: Risks of Having African Serval Cats as Pets

Choosing a pet to bring into your home is a huge decision. Because pets are not just display things, they are not objects that you can get from a store and leave in your home. They are not used to adorn your homes. Pets should not brought into one's home for selfish reasons — they are to be taken care of, fed, sheltered, played with, and loved. Pets have thoughts and feelings and should be considered as members of the family. You may get a pet through various means — purchasing one, being gifted with one, or taking one from an animal shelter. However you get a pet, you still need to be a responsible owner and ensure that you are capable of giving that pet a happy life.

Now, the search for the perfect pet may not be easy for some. For others, they want a pet that matches their lifestyle, one that is good for their kids, one that can keep them company. It is habitually thought that people look for pets wherein they find their match in personality—although this is often done unconsciously. Other people want to have pets that are rare breeds. There are some people who want exotic pets into their homes. The African serval cat is one such exotic pet. But along with the distinction and unique qualities that come with an exotic pet, are greater responsibilities and stricter requirements.

While you may find some African serval cats in some households, you should never forget that they are wild animals, no matter how domesticated they seem. Their inherent nature will always find a way to come forth—and with this knowledge, you should have an idea that there are risks to keeping an African serval cat as a household pet.

First of all, cats are amazing pets. There is no doubt that cats are some of the most wonderful furry creatures you can bring into your home. Nevertheless, not all cats can be fully accustomed to the human lifestyle, even the fully domestic ones. Thinking about this, wild cats can really pose some problems to their new owners. House cats may have behavioral problems, but they usually don't go beyond ruined couches or light scratches and bites. It may be slightly different with bringing wild cats home.

The African serval cat has many admirable qualities. That is the reason why some people choose this wild animal as an exotic pet to keep or breed. However, there really are not many of them. Many of the serval cats that you will find outside of their natural habitat are located in big cat rescues as well as zoos. The reason is simple: the African serval cat requires nurturing in specific environments and its inherent instincts can only be cultivated and satisfied in such environments, otherwise they will not thrive and may cause harm. In some states, owning a serval cat is prohibited. Other states require that an owner secure specific licenses before taking care of one. The reason for this prohibition is that there are risks that come with containing a serval cat.

If you are thinking of caring for this super cat as a domesticated pet, then read along before you make that big decision. Just as with bringing any pet home, there are a lot of things to take into consideration such as space, finances, time and, of course, your commitment. On top of all these factors, there is also the fact that the African serval cat is a wild animal hence, more risks and added requirements.

1. **African serval cats live in big habitats where they love to run around and explore in.** They need a place where they can hunt, swim and climb. They cannot be simply put in a cage or allowed to roam in a small yard. Their habitat should resemble that of their original home in order for them to thrive. This is costly to recreate and if you only have a small space to spare, your serval cat will not be able to use all its energy and become aggressive towards you. If you only let it stay indoors, then it won't be able to realize its natural instincts.

2. **African serval cats don't just eat regular cat food.** Don't expect to throw in some kibbles and other food mix and think that it will be satisfied nutritionally.

3. **African serval cats, even though domesticated, are still wild by nature.** You may be able to train them and they can be affectionate towards people, but don't expect it to be like your regular feline who loves to sit on your lap. There will be times it will act on its basic instincts.

4. **African serval cats hunt and go about during night to dawn.** So if you don't like to be disturbed by a big cat that is hunting or playing at 2:00 in the morning, then the African serval cat is not for you. Imagine a 40-pound cat jumping on you in the bed and starting you awake in the wee hours of morning. Imagine this happening every single day. There. Now do you still want a serval at home?

5. **African serval cats, no matter their gender, mark their territories.** Expect it to poo and pee all over your home, on your furniture and household items. Your serval cat may even mark you!

6. **The average life span of an African serval cat is estimated at 20 years.** That is a long time to have it as a pet, compared to your regular domesticated felines. While it can be good because you have a pet that can stay with you for almost a lifetime, this also means that you have the responsibility to care for this wild animal for a very long time. Are you up to the task? Then—yay!—get your serval now. If you are not up to long-term, then think twice and think hard.

7. **If you have gotten yourself an African serval cat and decide later on that it won't work for both of you, then you may find it hard to give it back.** Since they are wild animals and owning them will require legal restrictions, it is also difficult to renounce ownership. You will have to find individuals, shelters or groups that also have appropriate legal licenses to care for

them before you can give them your serval cat. It won't be easy to look for a new home for it.

8. If you really plan on giving it to a new owner, you should also realize that **African servals don't take on new owners very well**, especially if they have not been raised and fed from the bottle by humans from infancy. If you are thinking of giving your African serval cat to a zoo or a sanctuary, you will have to consider the fact that they may also already have serval cats in their care and they may not be accepted.

9. **If you have young children at home, having a serval cat is not recommended.** Like domesticated small cats, they may accidentally be rough with your children. African serval cats play using their claws and teeth, and if they see your children as prey or as a toy, it can be quite dangerous for your kids. They also have fast reflexes and are strong enough to knock your kids down when they play. They won't

necessarily mean harm, but their big size can be a disadvantage when playing with smaller humans.

10. **African serval cats, having an inherent instinct to play in wide open spaces in the wild, will also want to play hard in its new home with you.** They will leap and pounce, knocking over items in your home, scratching your furniture, tearing at your walls, crashing into appliances, and more. Can you handle it?

11. **The serval cats also love to chew on anything and there is the danger that it will ingest something it should not.** This will cause you to have frequent trips to the vet. Moreover, serval cats love to dig, as they look for rodents and other prey. Be prepared to find all sorts of scratches and holes in your home.

12. **You may think that declawing your serval cat may help**—especially if you have young kids at home and you don't want your furniture to be teared up. However, declawing is not recommended even when

your African serval cat is domesticated. In case in the future you decide to return the African serval cat to a sanctuary or a zoo, it will be at a disadvantage if it doesn't have claws. It won't have the ability to hunt, get its own food, or defend itself. Think about it.

13. **Your African serval cat will probably scatter his feces and urine almost everywhere in your home.** You can train it to do its business on litter boxes, but it won't be the same as domesticated smaller cats. Also, you will need a bigger litter box.

14. **You will have to keep your home safe and secure so that there won't be things that can pose a threat to your serval cat.** They are as curious as any cat, and couple this with their high-energy, they can get into all sorts of trouble, so it is best to "baby-proof" your home.

15. **Keep in mind that a serval cat has a 50% kill rate.**

When they pounce on their prey, they hold them for a while to weaken them with their weight. Then they will bite the prey on the neck to kill it. Now, this doesn't mean that your serval will kill you. But there is a risk when you have a pet that belongs to the best hunters in the cat family right in your home. You won't know if it is playing or acting on its instinct. Did you know that the kill rate of domestic cats is 10%? And even if your serval cat won't bite you, it can definitely give you a deeper scratch compared to a smaller domesticated cat when you play with it, because it is a strong wild animal.

In summary, you should remember that any animal will need to fulfill their natural instincts and it is no different with an African serval cat. It will play, pounce, dig, chew, scratch, growl, jump around, swim hunt and mark territory. You should be prepared to handle this emotionally and mentally so you won't get frustrated. Yes, your serval cat can become affectionate, too. Yes, they can act like other small domesticated cats, too. But keep in mind that they are, and will always be wild animals at heart. They don't like changing owners. They don't like too small spaces. They may need care when in captivity, compared to being able to live alone in the wild. Do not confuse having a large open space with being an efficient habitat for your African serval cat. Just because you have acres and acres of land, doesn't mean your serval cat will enjoy and thrive there. The space needs to replicate the serval's natural habitat, if you want your pet to be happy.

It is also good to consider that all across your country, there are many animal shelters that house different kinds of animals that have been rescued and need homes. How about thinking of them first before considering the serval cat along with its risks?

Now even after you read the risks involved in getting a serval cat, and you still want an exotic pet at home, then you are free to do so. You can visit the local zoo, a big cat sanctuary or a cat rescue facility.

Chapter Four: Different Instances Involving Servals Cats

Many people believe that serval cats cannot become pets. But you may hear differently from breeders. Who should you believe? No one can say for sure and it is always up to the owner to decide after taking everything into consideration. However, this book would like to be balanced about everything so even as it presents the amazing qualities of the African serval cats and different ways you can care for it at home, here is a compilation of some instances wherein serval cats have been said to be not so "safe to keep". It is up to the reader to weigh the pros and cons of bringing one home.

1. **An African serval can live up to twenty years in captivity.** If you think about it, it's quite a long time and a great joy that also involves great commitment. However, a lot of owners have kept their pet serval cats for only a year to a year and a half because they couldn't handle them. Specifically, previous owners didn't like how serval cats mark their territory, peeing on everything repetitively. You will have to face the same dilemma. Don't think that it is just about housebreaking. Serval cats are wild cats and it is in their nature to mark their territory. It is in their blood for thousands of years, no matter how domesticated their breed is. So if you don't like it, and you simply think you can house break your serval, you better decide properly.

2. **While regular domesticated cats have vaccines, there are no approved vaccines for exotic cats.** Your serval

cat may be at risk of getting infected by people or other animals that it gets in contact with.

3. **The African serval cat will hiss most of the time.** Some owners think that it is not fun to have a hissing cat all the time as it feels like their pet hates them, is afraid of them, or is ready to pounce on the.

4. **Serval cats stun their prey with their paws by slapping them senseless.** These are powerful cats. Sometimes, when they play with their human owners, they may slap or hit them with super - fast speed and great power that can cause real damage. This is also one of the reasons owners give up on their pet servals.

5. **African serval cats are awesome escape artists.** They can jump high, climb and even dig out of their enclosure. Given the above fact, one should also note that serval cats are great hunters. When they get loose, they can prove to be a real threat—to other pets, to the environment and to other humans even,

especially when they feel threatened. Even if they won't be a threat though, they will have to face the problem of surviving in a city and it can be a far cry from their natural habitat.

Following are some instances on record in which servals escaped their enclosures:

- Longview, WA. O January 2011, an African serval escaped from its owner's home and ran loose along different streets for a week. It began showing up in different people's backyards and gave people a scare as they thought it was a cheetah. The serval was caught using a trap. When it was returned to the owner, it was found out that it was illegally kept. The owner did not have permits and licenses.

- Cincinnati, OH. In December 2011, a serval was caught hovering over a domestic cat that it had killed. The serval was reported to have escaped nine days before it was finally caught.

- Tyrone Township, MI. The sheriff reported that they found an African serval cat in the town on July 2011, and brought it to the zoo. The owner did not come forward to claim it.

- Weedsport, NY. An African serval cat died on the highway as it was hit by a car after escaping from its enclosure through a fence gap on August 2011.

- Westtown, NY. On June 2013, a 35-pound male serval escaped a wire crate in an animal sanctuary. The serval cat was loose in the city for three days until it was finally caught sing a net.

- Morganton, NC. On August 2015, an owner reported that his pet serval went missing and could be roaming along Valdese and White Street. The 45-pound serval cat escaped a screened-in porch.

- Paterson, NJ. On March 2017, authorities tranquilized an African serval cat and brought it to the Wildlife Freedom in Wanaque. The serval was reported to have escaped its owner's apartment by climbing out of the window.

- Ontario, Canada. On July 2017 a serval cat was spotted roaming Forest Circle and Tiny Beach Road. It is feared that people may think it is a cheetah.

There are many other recorded incidences from way back to 2000. Some pet serval cats have escaped a couple of times and caught, there was even one pet serval that escaped four times! Most of the serval cats that escaped and were lost for at least a couple of days were found to be malnourished when they were re-captured.

In most instances, the serval cats either harmed domestic animals like cats and dogs or they got killed by running vehicles. In all the incidences where serval cats escaped their enclosures or homes, they triggered fear with the people in the neighborhood as they were perceived to be cheetahs that could harm or kill people.

In one specific instance in June 2000, in New York, a four-year-old boy had to go through plastic surgery after receiving a bite to his neck as well as puncture wounds in his face from a 40-pound serval that attacked him. The owner of the serval was just taking his pet for a walk and he had no idea that this would happen. They don't know what triggered the serval to act on his natural instinct. Even his owner suffered bite wounds on his hand and had to get several stitches.

Wild cats are wild cats, no matter how they are bred and domesticated. They will always have a wild instinct in their nature. You can choose to overlook this and face the risk. Or you can choose to consider this and keep yourself and other people around you safe. Nature has made a way to distinguish domesticated animals from wild ones. It is up to you to decide what to bring into your home. There is no right or wrong when it comes to keeping pets — the only thing that you can be reminded of, when it comes to taking in African serval cats as pets is for you to exercise responsible ownership.

Chapter Five: Responsible Ownership

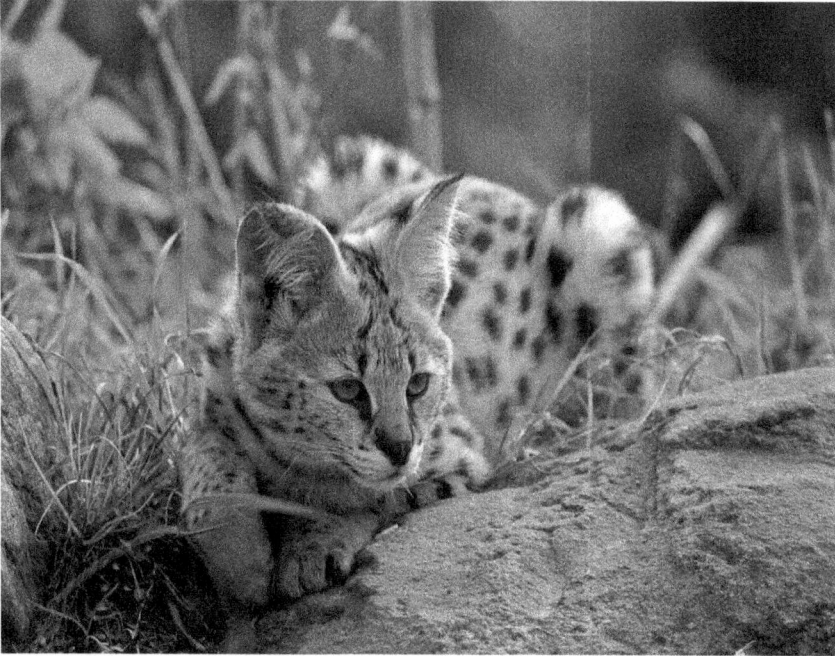

There is no doubt that serval cats can be fascinating pets. Once you get the proper knowledge about caring for an African serval cat as a pet, then you can give them proper care and understanding. With this, your serval will live a long, happy and safe life—and you will, too!

As an owner, you need to commit your time, efforts and even finances to caring for an African serval cat. You may even have to adjust your lifestyle. Responsible ownership means that you understand the different behaviors of serval cats and you find out and apply techniques and strategies on how to bond with your pet serval. You should also know the best practices of housing your serval cat, litter training, feeding, play and harness training requirements. Pet care for African serval cats is not as simple as pet care for dogs and small felines. They need different health care and even discipline methods.

First of all, you should consider that bringing an African serval cat home means you are considering it as a member of your family. It is okay to have expectations from it but it doesn't mean that you can have the same expectations as with other domesticated pets. As you start your life together, you will have to understand its breed and its special needs.

Your serval cat can become a bundle of joy—it will accept you as its owner, as the alpha, as a member of its pride. It can show you affection and loyalty. It can be trained and disciplined. Although with these things, it can be quite different than what you expect because, as it has been repeatedly said in this book, the African serval is a wild animal. You will never be able to completely domesticate it.

As a responsible owner, you need to accept this fact. Don't aim to be the first one to completely tame an African serval. You have to respect that your cat has a wild side. When you accept and respect this, you will get an understanding on how this wild side will replicate to you.

Now just because African serval cats are wild cats, it doesn't mean that you have to be scared and they will always be wild, vicious and aggressive towards you. It simply means that this side of them will remain as their characteristics because it has been used for thousands of years for survival. You simply cannot change that. Given this, you should remember that you should never yell at a serval cat. They will never, ever understand this behavior. No matter how upset, surprised or angry you are, do not shout at them—this will scare them away and can brutally damage whatever bond you have established with them.

Responsible ownership of pet serval cats mean:

- You treat them with love and respect. Even if they are wild animals, treat them with the same care, affection and esteem as you would domesticated pets. When serval cats feel this affection and regard, they will develop a strong bond with the people who take care of them. Serval cats are amazing; they are fiercely loyal and will treat you with deference that no other kind of cat can give you. They will protect you and care for you. They will crave for your attention and give you're their all. Serval cats will practically head butt you to be in their family or pride when they really, really like you.

- Learn all about its breed and needs. When you decide to accept the responsibility of caring for a serval cat, you accept the fact that since it is now in captivity, the serval is dependent on you for all its needs—this means food, water, shelter, medical attention and companionship. You cannot just bring one home and leave it to fend for itself, even though it can. You also cannot expect it to just adapt to whatever environment you put it in. As a responsible pet owner, you have to understand what kind of environment your pet will thrive in and do your best to provide that.

- You should understand its behavior and personality. All animals, wild or domesticated, have their own individual temperaments, quirks and personalities. Don't expect that a serval cat will naturally bond with you just because you are a good owner with a fun-loving personality. Not all cats are the same. Each has its own personality. One serval cat may bond with you forever; another may not care about you at all, for the whole time it is with you. Therein lies the dilemma. If the serval cat bond so strongly with you that you will have a hard time when you decide that you can't care for your pet anymore in the future. On the other hand, you don't want to have a pet that doesn't mind you and keep it for life! No one wants to spend 20 years with a serval cat that they cannot have any relationship with; no matter how beautiful or intelligent it is, especially as it will naturally depend on you for that long period of time. If you decide to give it to a new owner, the bonding with the new human is not guaranteed.

- When the time comes that you need to bring your pet serval to a new home, whether you are not able to care for it anymore or you need to relocate to a place you cannot bring it to, you will have to find it a new home. You should be very diligent in finding the best new home for your pet. Contact the breeder where you purchased it from or connect with a local serval community or a rescue. Life changes are understandable and it can be hard especially if you have a strong bond with your African serval cat. But there will be people who will support you and help you find a place that is safe and friendly for your serval cat. You should not be ashamed if you need to let it go. Similarly, if you really cannot care for it, or it was not as easy as you thought it would be, asking for help is so much better than letting your serval cat suffer or escape.

- Responsible owners have a back-up care plan for their pets, in the events of emergencies like a hospital stay or traveling to far places. You need to have someone who is ready to take care of your pet in the event that you simply cannot do it for the time being.

Understanding Serval Behavior

A responsible pet owner of a serval cat needs to understand that serval cats are smart. In the wild, they need this intelligence in order to survive and reproduce. Throughout the generations, the African serval cats have only grown smarter and smarter. Don't be surprised when your pet serval cat will learn to open doors! They can easily adapt to their environment and find ways to do what they want, whether to get food or escape. With this knowledge, the responsible pet owner secures his home as he would do so to protect a growing baby.

A serval cat is also naturally shy even though it is very active. So don't think that simply because you have a playful cat, that it will enjoy meeting new people every day. When they are playing, they can be quite focused and driven. Make sure that you understand this so that you don't disrupt them unknowingly and cause them to be aggressive. Here are some natural inclinations of your pet serval cat:

1. **They will run away from perceived danger.**

   Because of their intelligence, they will run away when faced with danger. So do not run after serval cats or chase them. They will perceive that you are a threat and you are out to hurt them. An owner should only run after his pet serval cat when it is an emergency. However, the best way to go about an emergency is to coax the serval cat to come to you instead of chasing it. You can do this by baby talking or cooing, using its favorite toy or coaxing it with a treat. Again, trying to catch a serval by chasing it will only cause it to further run away from you and probably into more danger, like a running vehicle.

2. African serval cats are cautious of strangers.

Even as the serval cat grows older, it won't prefer the company of strangers. They don't like anyone else that doesn't belong to their pride. The behavior of an African serval cat is that, in the wild, it is wary of other cats that come near their territory. They will either challenge it and -chase it away or run away from it.

If you are living with someone at home, make sure that both of you take the responsibility to care for and with your pet serval. While it naturally is a one-human pet, it can also bond with your partner or kids and include these people in its pride. However, if you will have visitors coming over, you will notice that your African serval cat will shy away and hide from them. It will not go out of hiding until the guests have left. This is natural and you should never force your pet serval to go out and meet your visitors. Don't bring it to display them. Your pet serval cat will become frightened. This can cause it to be emotionally or physically harmed. When you force it to go and meet people it doesn't like or is scared of, it will lose its trust in you. Moreover, warn your visitors not to chase your serval.

3. **Children should never be left alone with servals.**

   If you have children in your home, make sure that they are always supervised when they are around your pet serval. If your pet serval cat is afraid of children, this fear will stay with them forever. They don't like children's shrill voices, and they can easily distinguish an adult's voice from that of a child.

   It is highly recommended not to allow a serval cat near a child, not just for the safety and peace of your pet but most importantly for the child. African serval cats have very sharp claws and teeth, and they love to pounce when they are excited. They can easily hurt a young child. If you have older children, you can teach them to behave appropriately towards the pet serval. However, the danger of getting hurt is still there.

4. **Your pet serval won't like other pets very much.**

    While some servals can welcome playing with other animals, especially if they have been domestically bred, this only happens when they are young. As the African serval cat grows older, its natural instincts will kick in and it will become a solitary animal. It prefers to be alone and will resent company or feel it as a threat. Also, when it is an adult serval cat and you introduce a smaller animal to it, like a small puppy or kitten, then it can view the small animal as a chew toy or prey and hurt it.

5. **You can teach your African serval cat to trust you.**

    As with any pet that you are training, you can use food, treats, paly or toys to teach your pet serval cat to trust you. You need to show patience and avoid any negative responses. Your goal is to be friends with your serval cat. You can do this in the beginning by teaching it to directly feed from your hands. Your pet serval should feel that you are giving them something good whenever you reach for them, so that they don't run away.

You can also teach your serval to trust you and bond with you by laying down on the floor and playing with them using a favorite toy. When you watch over it while standing up, you will appear as a predator that it will be scared of. Do not tower over your pet but meet it at eye level so that it will feel the bond and not be dominated by you. When your pet serval is at ease with you, it will be comfortable playing with you, feeding from your hand, accepting your light touches, and even let you carry it. When it already trusts you, you can do other things with it even if you are sitting or standing up.

6. **Responsible pet ownership means you have lots and lots of patience.**

Raising pets is almost the same as raising kids. You need tons and tons of patience—bonding does not happen immediately. It takes time and effort. You need to be patient when talking with your pet serval—avoid yelling when it displays a behavior you don't like. A simple "No!" when said in a high-pitched voice, can frighten your pet. When they feel afraid, they will run away from you. You may never get their trust again, no matter how hard you try in the future. So be careful and be gentle. Watch your tone.

Moreover, you need to be careful about forcing yourself on your pet serval. Sure you want it to do something that is good for it, but forcing it won't help. It will only drive a wedge between you. Never hold your pet serval against its will. Never force-feed it. Never force it into the water. You get the picture—don't use force to get it to do something. It should come naturally. Else, you risk it not trusting you and you will never develop a bond with it, even if it stays with you for 20 years.

7. **Responsible pet owners understand the need to keep the place where the servals are housed as secure and safe as possible.** You should always keep your windows closed when you have serval pets roaming inside your house. You don't want them jumping out of the windows. Similarly, you should be careful where you place your furniture, cords, electrical wires, chemicals and breakables. Serval-proof the house so that nothing will entangle or fall on your pet serval. Your pet serval cat will perch on, stand up, and jump from anything in your house. They will sniff at and probably taste everything, even though it is poisonous. Remember, they don't know anything about chemicals. They are very playful and curious creatures that can ingest anything.

You can allocate a room as a den for your African serval cat so that it will not roam inside your home by itself when you are not home and at the same time it will not feel sad and confined.

Having an outdoor enclosure is great for your pet serval cat so that it can run around and still have ample shelter. You can install an enclosed catwalk so it can easily access your home. Don't forget to serval-proof even the outdoor enclosure. Remember the incident reports of serval cats escaping from their enclosures—you don't want it to happen to your pet.

How to Litter Train Your African Serval Cat

While your African serval cat will mark its territory by repeatedly scattering its poo and pee all over your house, since marking is its natural instinct. You can, however, litter train your serval cat.

You would need a larger than the standard litter box because the serval cat is bigger than most cats. You can get a box that is 16 x 24 x 18 inches in diameter. The serval cat needs enough room to do its business, so if you can get a bigger one that would be better. You have to provide two boxes: one is for defecation and the other is urination. Make sure that both boxes are always kept clean. Your pet serval cat will not do its business in a box that has been previously polluted with feces or urine. Clean the boxes after use, every single day. Here are some tips for you as well as other things you need to know:

1. **Your kitten will most likely be litter-trained already after you get it from a breeder.** But you still need to show it its own litter box where it can do its business. Also, your kitten won't cover up like other domestic cats do after they defecate.

2. **Talk to your kitten gently—never ever yell when litter training.** Make sure that your kitten understands the litter box is their "spot". In the wild, the African serval cat's natural instinct is to always do its business in the same spot. Point your kitten in the right direction using words. Don't shout or you will immediately create a rift between the two of you.

3. **Repetition is key.** When you see that your kitten is about to defecate or urinate but it is going to the wrong spot, gently pick it up and bring it to its litter.

Don't' scold the kitten about going to the wrong spot. Just pick it up, direct it and say "Here". You may have to do this a number of times until your kitten figures it out. When it is used to the litter box, it will naturally and faithfully go to the litter box to do its business.

4. **You should change the litter once a week and clean the box every day.** When a litter box is dirty, your serval cat will not do its business there and find somewhere else to defecate or urinate. When that happens, you should clean the area thoroughly to erase all scent. Additionally, do not use ammonia-based cleaning products to clean the "wrong spot" because the scent of ammonia will encourage your serval cat to go back to that same place.

5. **If you have other cats or other domesticated animals in your home, make sure that they have their own litter box separate from the serval cats.** Your pet serval is a solitary animal that wants its own territory,

it will not share. Even if it is a very big litter box. If you force it to use the same litter box, it won't go there at all and will just find another spot in the house to urinate or defecate, such as carpets, furniture or upholstery. Similarly, if your other domesticated pets do their business on your floor and furniture, your serval copy will follow suit. It is best to forbid al your pets at home to do that and train them all to use the litter box.

The Problem of Chewing

All kittens chew—whether they are domesticated small cats or wild cats—so it is good to provide your pet serval cat with chew toys made of hard plastic. Don't give your pet a soft plastic toy as it can chew on it and break it into smaller pieces using its sharp teeth. The plastic can be ingested by your kitten and block its intestine or make it choke.

Another problem you can have with chewing kittens is when they chew on electrical cords. They are at risk of ingesting the material or worse, get electrocuted if the cord is plugged on. To prevent your pet serval kitten from chewing on electrical cords, keep the cords hidden. If they cannot be hidden, the exposed cords should be sprayed with bitter apple spray so that your kitten will be discouraged from even getting near them. You can buy bitter apple spray from your local pet stores. You can e-spray frequently; they are not harmful to your pets. You can also use bitter apple spray on other items you want your pet serval to stay away from such as decorative pillows. Don't worry, as your pet serval matures, it will chew less and less.

Harness Training for Serval Cats

This is like leash training for dogs. You need to understand that you cannot take your African serval cat for a walk without a leash or harness. You need to train your serval cat to wear a harness at a young age. Do not use a collar because serval cats can easily get out of one quickly. So a harness is better suited.

Harness training your African serval cat is not easy. And it is not fun, especially in the beginning as your cat will not cooperate. It has a wild nature and of course will not like to be leashed. But it is not impossible, and with proper training, patience and time, you can soon convince your serval cat that this routine is something you prefer and something that is good for them.

Let your serval cat become accustomed to wearing its harness by strapping it on the body and letting your cat walk around the house. The next step is to strap the leash on the harness and allow your serval cat to roam the house or its cage freely. Make sure you watch your cat when its harness is attached because you don't want it to get hooked or entangled on something as it jumps. It could choke or get pulled down and break a bone.

When your serval cat is used to wearing the harness and leash that has no tension, you can train it to get used to the tension. Hold the leash lightly in the beginning until your pet serval gets accustomed to your pull. Guide your pet serval around the house using the leash and harness. When it is accustomed to it, you can take short walks just outside your home. Pretty soon, you and your cat can take walks along your neighborhood and you don't have to worry about it running away or getting lost. Often, your pet won't run away from you because it trusts you, but when you bring it outside, it may encounter many things that it would perceive as threats and try to run from them.

Before you get out of the house, however, check that the harness is secure. African serval cats are quite the contortionists. They are intelligent and will find a way to get out of the situations they don't like. It is best that you only go out for a walk when you are sure that your serval does not hate the harness. Do your very best to prevent your African serval cat from getting loose. When it does get loose and run away, they are faced with many potential dangers.

An unfamiliar neighborhood can be quite unfriendly to your pet serval. As it looks like a cheetah, many people will naturally be scared of it and may try to harm it. Other may try to catch it or play with it. It can get hurt or it can hurt others.

Disciplining Your African Serval Cat

You can reprimand your pet serval cat. They are intelligent creatures that understand the word "No." As long as you don't yell at it and just use a firm voice, your pet serval will get the picture and stop its behavior. Giving your pet a tap on the head as you say "No" is another good way to discourage wrong behavior such as biting. You can also try squirting it using a water pistol. If these methods won't work, you can just quit playing with your cat. It also understands that when you stop playing with it, it is doing something you don't like.

Since African serval cats are wild cats, they can be quite stubborn. You may have to say "No" to a certain wrong behavior several times before it finally understands and obeys. Repetition is necessary so that your pet serval will understand that you are the boss and you won't allow it to get its way and continue with a behavior you don't want. Again, you can use all kinds of communication with your serval except yelling. That is one thing they won't understand and it is something they deeply resent.

Serval Health Care

Responsible ownership means you know how to take good care of your serval cats, you are aware of the illnesses that they are prone to, and you offer them the best veterinary care you can give. There are specific exotic animal veterinarians and your pet serval cat needs one.

While most serval cats are very tough and strong, as an owner, your pet can also get sick and you should always be prepared for such instances. If you are not sure that your pet serval cat is well and safe, or you suspect that there is something wrong, do not hesitate to get veterinary care.

A serval cat cannot tell its owner how it is feeling or if it is sick. That is why you must be the one who is responsible for checking signs of illness, poor appetite or bad health. A responsible pet owner will be aware of the following:

- Diarrhea
- Vomiting
- Straining when urinating
- Drastic mood changes

If your pet serval has watery stool, it can be at risk of dehydration and may need intravenous fluids. When given immediate attention, diarrhea is not life-threatening. Often, you just need to change your cat's diet.

Don't forget to bring your serval cat to the vet for routine medical check-ups. They may need special care like need vaccinations, declawing, or neutering. By choosing the right vet for your serval cat, you can be sure that the vet will use only the right and tested vaccines on your serval cat—this means using vaccines that are from killed viruses. If the vaccine is made from live viruses, your serval cat can get sick and even die.

On the issue of declawing, you need to discuss this properly with a qualified veterinarian. It has been mentioned in this book that declawing can leave your serval cat at a disadvantage. But it can also offer an advantage to the owner: playtime will be friendlier and there will be less damage with furniture. If you plan on keeping your serval cat with you forever, maybe declawing is the best option for you. A qualified veterinarian can also offer advice on the best practice for neutering or spaying your pet serval cat, especially if you have more than one and they are of different genders.

Chapter Six: Conservation: The Hunter is Being Hunted

Wait and see…. that is the hunting strategy of the African serval cat. They will take their time and wait patiently and quietly in tall grasses and use their large ears to listen to the sound of approaching prey. When they are sure, they will pounce on the unsuspecting animal. African serval cats have a 50% hunting rate, the best in the big cat family. Their method of waiting and seeing before pouncing is both efficient and quick. When they pounce, they will use their full body weight to trap their prey then deliver a bite to its neck.

Chapter Six: Conservation: The Hunter Being Hunted

The African serval cat is famous for its hunting style and amazing hearing. It is believed to be the most successful predator among all cats, big and small. However, despite its great a talent for hunting, it seems that the hunter is the one being hunted and faces the danger of losing many of its kind.

In Africa, many serval populations have reportedly declined over the years. Even though most of the species, except one, are not yet considered endangered species, their conservation is still a big issue. One subspecies of the serval cat, the North African *Leptailurus serval constantinus* is now endangered.

The African serval cat is a beautiful wild animal. So beautiful that poacher hunts it for its fur. To produce one beautiful coat, a lot of servals are killed. It is sad that many animals have to die to dress up one person. Fortunately, wearing coats made from animal skin has lost its popularity. The African serval cats are also hunted for its meat as well as for sport. Other factors that lead to the decline in serval cat populations are global climate change and loss of habitat.

Still another reason is exotic pet trade: more and more people want to own exotic cats. Poachers hunt and import serval cats to breeders. Serval cats are sold at a hefty price on the black market.

In some places in Africa, the serval cats are hunted not for fun or money, but because they attack people's poultry farms. Nevertheless, you can't find any more African serval cats in highly populated areas. They keep to the quiet savannas.

The question is: will the awesome hunter survive being hunted itself? That remains to be seen. Meanwhile, there are many organizations that aim to protect the serval cats from being endangered, much more being extinct. They do all kinds of awareness campaigns so that the plight of the serval cats will be addressed and wildlife can be preserved. They also offer some solutions to address the protection of serval cats such as the following:

1. Engaging wildlife scouts.

   The African Wildlife Foundation, a great organization in the continent, aims to work with the African communities in protecting the wildlife. They employ the help of those who live near the wildlife as scouts and provide them with the necessary tools to do their task. This includes vehicles and GPS devices. When there are scouts in the area, they protection of wildlife is ensured in specific areas. Moreover, the organization provides employment opportunities to the locals.

2. Promote symbiosis.

   In a symbiotic environment, both parties get benefits. This is the kind of environment that many wildlife preservation organizations promote. They incentivize communities as they protect wildlife. For instance, by refraining from hunting wildlife and using them for products, the local community is trained to agricultural techniques and other sustainable methods that can provide economic security.

3. Education and public awareness.

The Serval Conservation and Educational Refuge is another organization that aims to protect the serval cats in particular. They provide education to people regarding husbandry of servals. They also provide a shelter for rescued servals, care for them then rehome them. Educating people about wildlife conservation is the first step to caring for the wild animals. People should realize the importance of balance and caring for nature's animals, and not just focus on gaining profit.

Some non-profit organizations, like the Cat Conservation Trust and the Feline Conservation Federation, create public awareness by publishing research and doing talks. Other organizations that do the same include Honda, Rare Species Fund, Taxidermy Africa and Karoo Taxidermy.

4. Habitat preservation.

A lot of serval populations have declined because the big cats have lost their natural homes. Burning of grasslands and global climate has had a bad effect on these amazing animals. Serval cats prefer areas that are near water sources and places where grass grows tall. As water sources get dried up and grasslands disappear because they are being used for farming, the servals lose their homes and their numbers dwindle. Many organizations work to promote preservation of natural habitats.

5. Reintroduction of serval cats

The serval cat was completely extinct from the Eastern Cape, Africa in the last century. This happened because of hunting as well as the loss of their natural habitat. However, the Kariega Foundation and the Kariega Game Reserve worked together and reintroduced the serval cats in the conservation area at Eastern Cape. The Kariega Serval Reintroduction Program ws successful and it has promoted the growth of the serval population in Eastern Cape. First two males were released, followed by two females. These two pairs were set up in the area in large outdoor, natural enclosures and were cared for by volunteers. They settled well in the

reserve and gave birth to kittens. When the kittens

matured, they were released as well and were able to

establish their own territories. Now, there is a

growing serval community in the area.

In many places, there are wild cat sanctuaries that
provide a haven for rescued wild cats as well as those that
their owners cannot take care of anymore. Often, people will
buy exotic cats because it is popular and to entertain
themselves, but they soon discover that this commitment of
caring for an exotic cat is not for them. They bring their pets
servals to a sanctuary. Many sanctuaries, like the Wildlife
Sanctuary in Minnesota, is a no-kill shelter and aims to
provide the most natural environment to the animals it
saves. They also promote their cause through sharing the
stories of the animals in their care as well as through
educating the public about the condition and attitudes of the
animals in the sanctuary.

Another organization, the Wildlife Big Cats, focuses on saving wildlife by using science and inspiring people all over the world about the importance of big cats. They aim to stop illegal poaching. They also partner with other wildlife conservation organizations, such as the African Conservation Fund, to provide intelligence, offer training to rangers and help enforce wildlife laws.

You can do your share! If you love serval cats as much as you say or think you do, owning a pet serval may not necessarily be as bad. But you can also take part in the conservation of these beautiful, intelligent cats by checking in with wild cat conservation groups and finding out ways you can help.

If you do not like keeping serval cats as pets and you are opposed to their hunting and breeding, make sure to report to the proper authorities if ever you find out people or businesses that are involved in the black market of importing serval cats and serval cat meat or skin. Wildlife, especially big cats need protecting and they are worth fighting for!

Chapter Seven: Serval Cat for a Pet? Why Not?

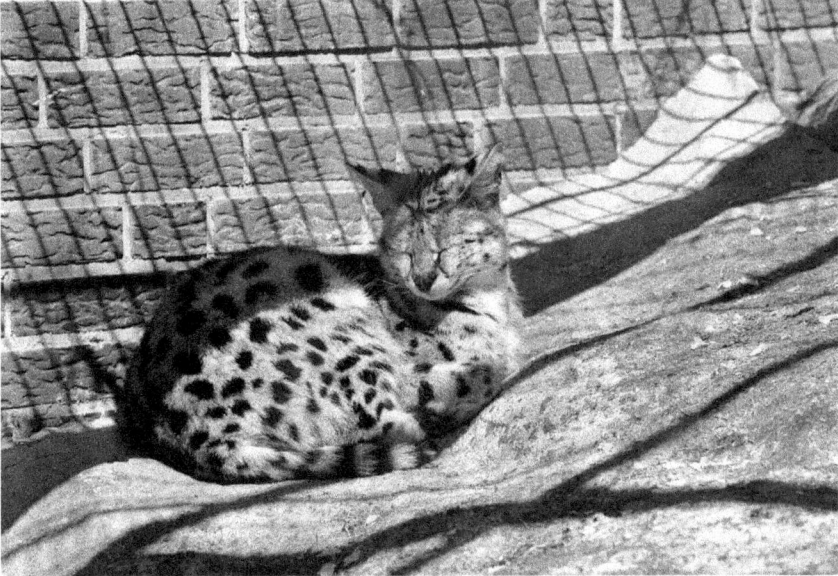

Getting yourself a pet is one if the best things you can do in life. It is no different with bringing an African serval cat home. Here are some of the reasons why:

1. You get companionship. If you are a single young adult, you can feel loneliness big time. This despair can be an unwanted companion that brings with it complications to your mental, physical and emotional health. As you age, you long for the company of someone—and it can be an animal that will be ready

to stay with you through different times, depend on you for their needs, and surprisingly offer affection when you need it most.

When an African serval cat gets a liking towards you and trust you, it will count you as one of its own. It will adopt you—and with that it will offer you all of its affection and attention. It will respect you like no other and listen to your instructions. It will make time to play with you and understand what kinds of behavior you want it to display.

2. You can develop a routine. Do you know that routine can bring a sense of purpose in your life? It is true— the structure that comes with the routine of caring for your pets will improve your mental health as well. Maybe you don't want to get out of bed early or you don't want to go for a walk or run. Your pet can make you do these things.

With an African serval cat, you may have to do a lot of running, walking and playing. You will also do a lot of cleaning and replenishing of supplies. It can be a lot of work to think of, but when you get yourself in a routine, you won't even think about it and you will just enjoy doing things for and with your pet serval.

3. You get exercise you never would do on your own. You will also get out of the house more. Not many people like to take walks even though it is good for the health. An exercise routine, even if it is as simple as jogging, can be easy to skip. When you have a pet serval cat with you, with its playful and active personality, you will be kind of forced to train it on a harness and take it for walks or runs. Not only is it good for your pet, it also provides great benefits for you. Exercise can now be part of your daily plans! Moreover, you will be able to get out more. You can stop living a sedentary lifestyle—remember, it can bring about so many illnesses you can otherwise avoid by moving around not only for walks, but when you go visit the veterinarian or the groomer.

4. Even big animals can help diminish stress.

   Many people think that only furry, huggable creatures can help you cope with stress. That is essentially untrue. Large animals such as serval cats can also be a source of relaxation. Having them feed from your hands or sits on your lap and letting you stroke them can be quite calming. African serval cats are highly affectionate once you have gained their trust and when you get home after having a bad day, you can just call your pet over and experience a sense of relaxation as you play with it or even just sit beside it.

5. You can make new friends.

   As a pet owner, it is ideal for you to find other pet owner of the same kind that you can have shared activities with or just so you can talk about different things that involve caring for your pet. The same can be true with owning a pet serval cat. You can connect with other people that care for African serval cats in your local community or even online!

Having a serval cat for a pet can help you make meaningful connections. Who knows, if you are single, you may meet your partner in life at the next meet-up of serval cat pet owners? Your serval cat can be your matchmaker! For introverts, it can be hard to meet new people, let alone make friends. But when there is a common ground like a pet, it can be an amazing icebreaker.

6. You can establish new interests.

   Having a dog or a cat is not new. Maybe you want something more interesting or you want to learn something you have never tried before. Then getting a pet serval cat is a good path. Learning all you can do for your pet will open your mind to greater knowledge.

   If you cannot afford to get a pet serval for a pet of your own, you can volunteer in big cat sanctuaries, too. Spend time with these amazing animas and support the cause of the foundation while you're at it. New activities bring a can new joy to your life.

7. You have someone who depends on you, someone you need to take care of.

   Caring for someone can be purposeful. When you own a pet, it is entirely dependent on you. You can't just buy it then leave it in an enclosure to fend for itself. You will have to care for it. This fulfills a need in you to be useful, to be of value. It is especially helpful for people who have kids who are already grown up or those that have retired from their careers. They no longer feel valued and needed. To have someone depend on them for their survival, can boost their confidence and give them a sense of purpose and pride. It is very satisfying to care for an African serval cat—especially when it reciprocates your attention and affection.

Bringing home an African serval cat, and caring for it, is much like investing in life—both yours and the pet's. As long as you have the serval cat in your care, you are committing to being involved in its life. As you grow older, you will realize that your life is made richer not by accumulating wealth or satisfying yourself, but by giving of your life to someone or something, like a pet.

In summary, here are some of the amazing facts that attract people into getting an African serval cat for a pet:

- African serval cats are not on the endangered species list.
- African serval cats have been in Egyptian households from ancient times. They have been popular then and are still quite popular now.
- African serval cats are exotic animals and having an exotic animal for a pet is great, even though it may have special requirements.
- African serval cats are solitary creatures and they develop a one-human bond.

- The African serval cat can weigh as such as 50 pounds and is a preferred choice for those who love big cats. Not as big as the tiger but not as small as domestic cats.

- African serval cats are intelligent big cats. They can be litter-trained and harness-trained, among other things.

- African serval cats are very attractive with their huge ears and beautifully-colored coat. The back of their ears have a solid black color and has a large white dot.

- African serval cats are great hunters. They hide in tall grasses and live near watery areas where they find their prey.

- African serval cats have a varied diet of fish rodents, small reptiles, frogs, crabs, large insects and birds. They are quite amazing at hunting because they find many ways to get their prey using their skills, such as catching a bird in flight, clawing for fish in the water and getting a rodent out of its hole in the ground.

- African serval cats are capable of different vocalizations such as growls, purrs and high-pitched calls.

- African serval cats are have been used to produce hybrids such as the savannah cat. This cat is a cross between the serval breed and some domestic cats, and they are easier to take care of.

- The African serval cat can run with a speed of more than 50 miles an hour.

- African serval cats are popular for their supersonic ears that they utilize for hunting prey.

- The African serval cats' native habitat is in the savanna grasslands of central and southern Africa.

- African serval cats require a heavily lush habitat that has a water source like a rover, lake or stream. In captivity, this habitat should be recreated well.

- African serval cats are up and about during dawn and dusk. They hunt and play during this time.

- African serval cats can leap up to ten feet in a vertical way. They can even clear a span of twenty feet and beyond.

- Like most cats, African serval cats can climb trees, either for fun and exercise or to escape predators.

- African serval cats are chased by lions, wild dogs, hyenas and leopards as well as humans.

- African serval cats can help the community where they live by keeping the population of destructive rodents very low. Rats are their most favorite meals,

- African serval cats love to mark territories and can do the same thing even in captivity. They mark spots with urine or feces. They can also leave scratch marks. Pet owners often think of ways to discourage this behavior or to redirect it.

- It is hard to breed African serval cats on your own. In the wild, the females use tall grass as nests and they don't den like other big cats. This is not easy to replicate in a small home or small enclosure.

- Characteristics of the African serval cat include: low levels of friendliness whether with kids or other pets, very low tolerance for visitors, medium level of showing affection, high levels of energy and playfulness, and very high intelligence.

African serval cats can be lovely pets, just decide to give caring for it a lifetime commitment of love and care. It can be challenging at times and not too easy on your wallet. But then again, your dedication in bringing one into your home will eventually pay off, sooner than you think.

Conclusion

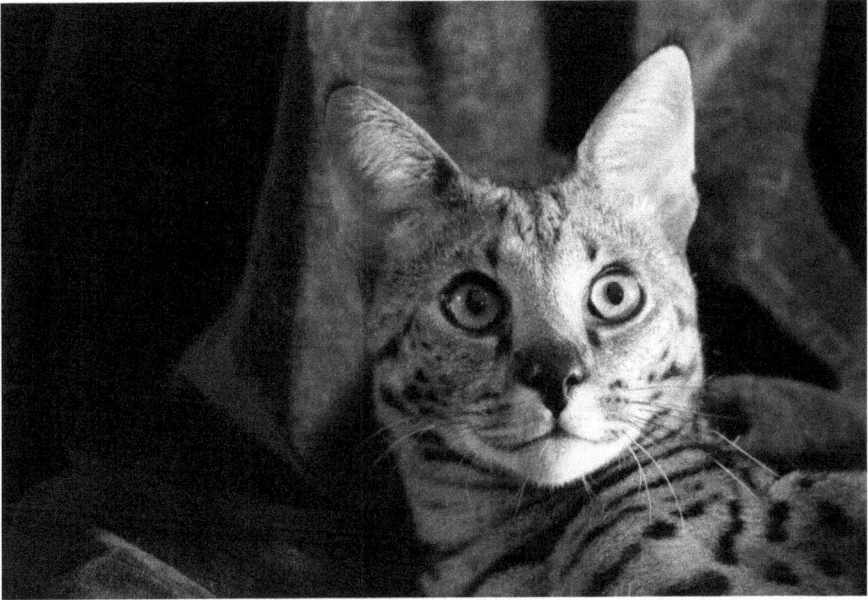

One of the best known wild cats is the African serval cat. It is the breed that is used to create the popular savannah cat that many people have for pets. The African serval cat is a very attractive cat. It looks fierce like a cheetah, but is quite beautiful with its large ears. Their long legs are also part of their charm. Add their intelligence, their natural hunting abilities and their long lifespan, this big cat is probably one of the most amazing and most well-loved wild cats in the world. That is why many people want to have it for their pet.

Throughout the book, you have learned the pros and cons of adopting an African serval cat for a pet. Caring for a pet is never easy—even if it is just a pet goldfish. But despite the lifelong commitment of time, effort, patience and finances, bringing a pet home is ultimately rewarding. There is no monetary value to the joy, loyalty and companionship that a loving pet can bring into your life.

Domesticated serval cats have been around for many, many years. It is not a novel thing to own a serval for a pet. In fact, African serval cats were the very first wild cats to be domesticated. They were kept in a family and they roamed freely in human households. And they thrived very well. If you are really attracted to the African serval cat and you know that you can take good care of it, then go for it. It won't be an easy journey, especially in the beginning.

You may be one of those in the statistics that return their pet servals to sanctuaries after only a year because you cannot handle the pressures of caring for one. Or you can be one of those few who managed to stay with their servals for decades.

You need to remember that these serval cats are wild cats, and while domesticated they still possess their natural wild tendencies. Can they be truly happy living with people? Yes, in some ways and no, in other ways. There is a delicate balance. Just as you can question whether it is good for a fish to live in a big aquarium instead of in a real body of water. Often, even though you can replicate its natural habitat, the wild cats will still be looking for something, as it is inherent to them.

You need to take care that your pet African serval cat will not get out of its enclosure. You don't want it to get lost in unfamiliar territories. Especially if you live in the city, your pet serval cat is at risk of being run down by a vehicle or being shot by someone who thinks it is a cheetah. A serval cat that gets loose can harm small animals in the area as it perceives them to be prey. There have been many recorded incidences of escapes happening, and most of the time, it did not end well for the African serval cat. It is not always the

owner's fault that the serval cat gets out from its home —
these cats are highly intelligent and will do anything out of
curiosity. Because of its skillfulness, it can even get its body
out of a harness!

Now, with all the reports on owners losing their pet
servals as they managed to escape or those that return their
African serval cats to sanctuaries because they could not care
for them anymore, you may feel that this venture may not be
feasible to begin with. That is not true. While it is not easy to
care for one, this doesn't mean that you cannot be successful
with keeping an African serval cat for a pet. You definitely
can.

As long as you are a responsible owner, there is no
need to worry. Give it the right nutrition, home, veterinary
care and affection and you are on the right track to being a
great serval cat owner. You can even train it. Responsible
ownership means that, when the time comes that you really
cannot care for it anymore, you will go and find it the best
new home where it will be taken care of.

Conclusion

The African serval cat can be one of the best long-term companions you can ever have in your life. But remember, there is no shame when you absolutely have to give it to a sanctuary or a zoo for all the right reasons. It means that you are a responsible pet owner because you are looking out for the best interests of the animal. You can choose to keep it with you and it can suffer because you don't have enough resources or time as your lifestyle permits—or you can bring it to a place where it will thrive and be happy. So take that chance, and make the best decision when it is needed.

Moreover, you need to understand that you can never really "own" a serval cat. While you can claim that you "have" a domesticated wild cat at home—in reality, the serval cat really owns you. It adopts you into its pride. You don't rule over it. Your African serval cat can depend on you for many things such as food, shelter and affection, but you are not its lord or master. It is affectionate to you because it trusts you. It sometimes wants to keep you for itself, and sometimes it reluctantly shares you with other people or other servals that live with it.

Conclusion

Having a serval cat at home will be one of the most amazing journeys you can undertake. Make sure you do your research well before you make that important commitment.

Photo Credits

Page Photo by user Kaz via Pixabay.com,

https://pixabay.com/en/serval-animal-cat-wild-wildlife-220493/

Page Photo by user skeeze via Pixabay.com,

https://pixabay.com/en/savannah-cat-closeup-feline-hybrid-518134/

Page Photo by user sipa via Pixabay.com,

https://pixabay.com/en/servals-small-cat-wildcat-predators-330117/

Page Photo by user sipa via Pixabay.com,

https://pixabay.com/en/serval-small-cat-wildcat-predators-330059/Page Photo by user via Pixabay.com,

Page Photo by user 3342 via Pixabay.com,

https://pixabay.com/en/serval-small-cat-wildcat-predators-84082/

Page Photo by user skeeze via Pixabay.com,

https://pixabay.com/en/two-servals-felines-cats-big-fur-597592/

References

Serval Cats – The Spruce Pets

https://www.thesprucepets.com/serval-cats-1238152

Serval – San Diego Zoo Organization

https://animals.sandiegozoo.org/animals/serval

Servals Not Pets – Big Cat Rescue

https://bigcatrescue.org/servals-not-pets/

African Serval – Krugerpark.co.za

http://www.krugerpark.co.za/africa_serval.html

Should I Get Serval Cats? – Petful.com

https://www.petful.com/cat-breeds/should-i-get-serval-cat-risks/

Serval Cats Fact Sheet – Tenikwa.com

http://tenikwa.com/serval-fact-sheet/

Wildlife Conservation Serval – AWF.org

https://www.awf.org/wildlife-conservation/serval

Serval Cats – AnimalComer.co.uk

https://animalcorner.co.uk/animals/serval/

African Serval Information – Animal World

http://cats.animal-world.com/ExoticCats/information/african_serval_informati on.php

Serval Cats – Animal Facts Encyclopedia

https://www.animalfactsencyclopedia.com/Serval-cat.html

Serval Cats – A – Z Animals.com

https://a-z-animals.com/animals/serval/

Should You Invite a Wildcat Into Your Home – BarklyPets.com

https://barklypets.com/blog/should-you-invite-a-wildcat-into-your-home/